200 SUPER-FUN, SUPER-FAST
MATH STORY PROBLEMS

Quick & Funny Math Problems That Reinforce Skills in Multiplication, Division, Fractions, Decimals, Measurement, and More

BY DAN GREENBERG

D1556483

SCHOLASTIC
PROFESSIONAL BOOKS

New York ★ Toronto ★ London ★ Auckland ★ Sydney
★ Mexico City ★ New Delhi ★ Hong Kong ★ Buenos Aires

Cover design by Hera Marashian
Interior design by Grafica, Inc.
Cover and interior illustrations by Mike Moran

ISBN 0-590-37894-5

1 2 3 4 5 6 7 8 9 10   40   08 07 06 05 04 03 02

TABLE OF CONTENTS

INTRODUCTION

Liven up your math class with *200 Super-Fun, Super-Fast Math Story Problems!*

These laugh-out-loud mini-story problems —one for each day of the school year—are guaranteed to fire up students' imagination and whet their appetite for math. As this book's title implies, math is enjoyable, even super-FUN!

Math also applies to kids' lives. For example, if they wanted to join a CD club, how can they tell which club has the better deal? Is it the club that sells CDs for $10 each or the one that offers CDs for $12 each, with every fifth CD for free? *(Answer: It depends on how many CDs they plan to buy!)* Kids will easily relate to the story problems in this book where math is used in shopping, watching sports, going to the movies, following a recipe, or doing the laundry!

Kids will build and practice skills in addition, subtraction, multiplication, division, fractions, decimals, measurement, graphing, time, money, and so much more. The problems in this book will help you meet the National Council of Teachers of Mathematics (NCTM) curriculum standards.

How to Use This Book

The math story problems are arranged monthly, from September to June. Each month contains 20 quick problems that tie in to that month's seasonal theme. However, don't feel that you have to follow the sequence of problems as we've presented them in the book. If you need to teach a specific skill at a certain time, feel free to pick the problems that suit your current needs.

Here are more suggestions for using this book:

★ Use the problems to jumpstart your math class, either to introduce a new problem-solving skill or to review previously learned skills.

★ You may want to copy individual problems onto the board or display them on an overhead projector.

★ You can also assign the problems as homework or for extra credit.

★ Always encourage students to "show their thinking." How did they come up with the solution? Invite students to discuss their strategies—often, there are different ways to arrive at the same solution. Students will benefit from hearing their classmates' strategies.

★ Invite students to make up their own word problems for classmates to solve. Students can post them on a classroom bulletin board or in the math center.

Enjoy!

SEPTEMBER

PATTERNS

Hurricane September

In the Gulf of Mexico, September is hurricane season. Hurricanes are named in alphabetical order, with alternating male and female names. The first four hurricanes for 2002 were given these names:

Arthur, Bertha, Cristobal, Dolly

What might be a good name for the 12th storm of the season?

ADDITION

See You in September

Wendy needs to mail her letter from camp, but she has only a 14¢ stamp. To mail the letter, she needs 34-cents' worth of postage.

Which stamps should Wendy add to make a total of 34 cents? Find two different ways.

ESTIMATION

The Amazing Colossal Dinosaur Problem

Over the summer, Walter visited the Dinosaur Museum and saw the Amazing Colossal Dinosaur Bone.

Walter is 4 feet tall. How long would you estimate the Amazing Colossal Dinosaur Bone to be?

MEASUREMENT

Hoppy's Climb

Hoppy the frog is hopping up a tilted log that is 13 feet long. On each jump, she moves 5 feet forward. Then she slides back 2 feet before jumping again.

How many jumps will it take for Hoppy to jump off the end of the log?

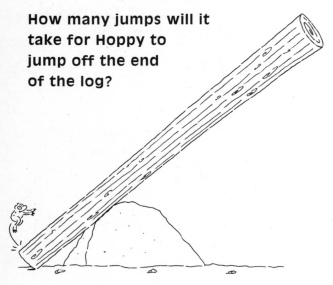

TIME

First Day of School

School in the Metro area starts on the day after Labor Day. Labor Day always falls on the first Monday in September.

When is the earliest date on which school will start? The latest date?

(Hint: You might want to use a calendar to solve this problem.)

PROBLEM SOLVING

Acorns Away!

Doris, Boris, and Natasha are squirrels.

To them, acorns are as precious as pearls.

"Excuse me," says Boris,
  while climbing a tree.

"But don't you have more
  acorns than me?"

"Oh, my!" cries Natasha.
  "I'm afraid that's true.

Now what in the world
  is a squirrel to do?"

How can each squirrel get the same number of acorns?

Use acorns, coins, or other items to solve the problem. Move items until each pile has the same number of items.

MONEY

School Supplies

Suvi has $2.00 to buy school supplies from the Supply Depot.

The Supply Depot		
Item	**Cheapo**	**Deluxe**
Pencil	10¢	49¢
Pen	35¢	98¢
Notebook	89¢	$1.29

What is the most he can spend if he gets one of each type of item?

How much change will he receive?

NUMERICAL REASONING

Half Way

*It's birthday time—and it's easy
  to remember*

That our three favorite squirrels

Have birthdays in September.

*The 10th is Natasha's birthday;
  the 20th is for Boris.*

So let's sing them both

A hearty birthday chorus.

*Happy birthday, dear squirrels.
  Best wishes to you.*

By the way, Doris's birthday

Falls between the other two!

Doris's birthday falls midway between the birthdays of Natasha and Boris.

On what date is Doris's birthday?

FRACTIONS

Bumble Bees Bash Blazers

In their first basketball game, the Bumble Bees scored 90 points and won. Florence scored 30 of those points.

What fraction of the team's total points did Florence make?

Day 10

LOGICAL REASONING

Goin' to Town

Rey went to town and did three things: he got a haircut, ate an ice-cream cone, and bought a new shirt. Use the following clues to figure out the order in which Rey did each thing:

★ Rey ate his ice-cream cone as soon as he bought it. He also put on the new shirt as soon as he bought it.

★ When Rey got home, he saw that his old shirt had an ice-cream stain on it.

★ Rey's new shirt had no ice-cream stains but it did have some barber-shop hairs on it.

What did Rey do first?

Second?

Third?

Day 11

MONEY

Rich and Penny

"I'm rich," says Rich.

"No, you're not," says Penny.

"You have 5 coins.

That's not very many.

Twenty-seven cents

Is all you've got.

You may be Rich,

But rich you're not!"

Rich has 27 cents in dimes, nickels, and pennies.

How many of each coin does he have?

Day 12

PATTERNS

Bagby's Bags

Ginnie collects bags from Bagby's Bag Store. She stores her bags inside her other bags. Ginnie has 1 giant Bagby's bag that has 2 large bags in it. Each large bag has 2 medium-sized bags in it. Each medium-sized bag has 2 small bags in it.

How many bags does Ginnie have in all?

ADDITION
Magic Square

Complete this magic square by filling in the empty spaces. Every row, column, and diagonal of three numbers should add up to 24.

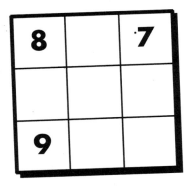

TIME
Getting Darker Every Day

On September 21, the sun sets at exactly 6:00 P.M. in Fargo, North Dakota. Each week after that, it gets dark 5 minutes earlier. For example, on September 28 the sun sets at 5:55 P.M. On the following week the sun sets at 5:50 P.M.

At this rate, at what time will the sun set on December 21, the shortest day of the year?

GRAPHS
Crunch-aroo to You

Crunch-aroo Cereal takes part in a "Box Tops for Books" program, in which prizes include "Crunch-aroo Kids" books.

★ **Anyone who collects more than 30 box tops wins a "Crunch-aroo Kids" mystery book.**

★ **The top three collectors in the class also win a Crunch-aroo T-shirt.**

★ **Anyone who collects more than 80 box tops wins a Crunch-aroo Plush Toy.**

How many kids won a mystery book?

Who won a T-shirt?

Which kid won a book and a plush toy but not a T-shirt?

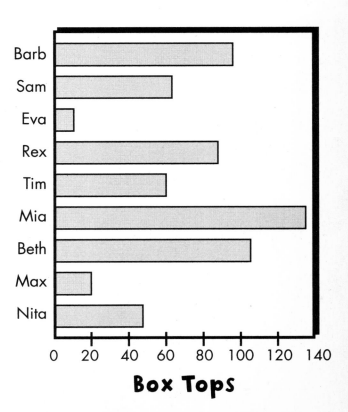

Box Tops

GEOMETRY

Squares and Rectangles

Trace as many different squares and rectangles as you can in this shape.

How many can you find?

FRACTIONS

Autumn Carrot Cake

Thom and Rona are baking an Autumn Carrot Cake without a written recipe. They need to add baking powder to the mixture.

Thom says, "We need more than 1/2 cup of baking powder."

Rona says, "We need less than 3/4 cup of baking powder."

Can both bakers be correct? Give an amount between 1/2 and 3/4.

PROBABILITY

Sock Sense

Rennie put 2 striped socks, 2 polka-dot socks, and 2 white socks into the dryer.

If he pulls out one polka-dot sock, what are the chances that the next sock he pulls out

★ **will be polka-dot?**

★ **will be striped or white?**

LOGICAL REASONING

Addition Puzzle

Find the digit that each letter stands for. Write the correct digits in the spaces provided.

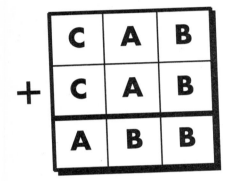

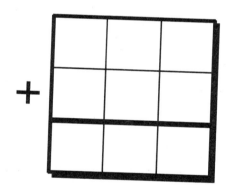

Hint: Start with the right side of the sum. If B + B is equal to B, then what digit must B be? Once you know B, replace other B's with the correct digit.

MAPS

Jennie's Bike Tour

Jennie rode through three towns on her bike trip: Albion, Brentwood, and Clarksville. She can't remember exactly how the towns were arranged. But she can remember the following facts:

★ Albion and Brentwood are 30 miles apart.

★ Clarksville and Albion are 10 miles apart.

★ Clarksville is 40 miles from Brentwood.

★ All three towns are arranged in a straight line.

How were the three towns arranged? Draw a map.

OCTOBER

MIXED OPERATIONS

Dean's Spooky Halloween Band

Welcome, everyone!
My name is Dean.
Would you like to hear some music
On this night of Halloween?

Hey, if you don't mind,
We'll be wailing and moaning,
Screaming and screeching,
Grunting and groaning.

So sit right down,
Kick up your feet,
And listen to a musical
Halloween treat!

Dean's band will play four 6-minute spooky songs, three 5-minute weird songs, and four 3-minute eerie songs.

How many minutes will his band play in all?

MONEY/PROBLEM SOLVING

Haunt Me!

Winnie, Vinnie, and Pat worked at the Haunted House last week.

★ **Winnie dressed up as The Hideous Slime Ghoul and made 3 dollars more than Vinnie.**

★ **As The Moaner, Pat's job was to stand on the roof and make horrible moaning sounds. Pat earned 5 dollars less than Vinnie.**

★ **Vinnie worked as Vinnie the Friendly Vampire. He made $9.**

How much did each worker make?

DIVISION

Dean's Halloween Band on Tour

Dean's band and all their fans are going on the road! Forty people plan to go on the trip in vans that hold 8 people each.

How many vans do they need?

FRACTIONS

The Grasshopper and the Ant

In October, the Grasshopper and the Ant were both searching for food in the field.

"I found 33 seeds," said Ant. "I'm going to store them for the winter."

"I, too, found 33 seeds," said Grasshopper. "I'll eat 1/3 of them for breakfast, 1/3 for lunch, and 1/3 for dinner."

"You'll be sorry," said Ant.

"We'll see," said Grasshopper.

How many seeds will Grasshopper eat for each meal?

TIME

The Columbus Files

On August 3rd in 1492,
Columbus sailed the ocean blue.
Three ships sailed many miles each day
Until finally they heard the captain say:
"Land ho!" And then the sails unfurled.
And soon they were looking
Upon a whole new world.

Columbus's ships landed in San Salvador on October 12, 1492.

How many days did Columbus's ships travel?

PATTERNS

Infinite Bowling

"I like bowling with 10 pins," Chloe says. "But why stop with just 10?"

Chloe keeps adding rows of pins to the basic pattern. For example, she added 5 pins for the 5th row.

If she bowls with 5 rows of pins, how many pins will there be in all?

Six rows?

Seven rows?

Row	Number of Pins in Each Row	Total Number of Pins
1	1	1
2	2	3
3	3	6
4	4	10
5		
6		
7		

MIXED OPERATIONS

Drop Pumpkin Pie

Dan's famous Drop Pumpkin Pie recipe simply calls for 2 pumpkins to make 4 pies. Dan drops the pumpkins from the roof of his house to soften them up. Dan needs to bake 20 pies for the Columbus Day celebration.

How many pumpkins will he need?

FRACTIONS

Monday Night Football

October is that special time
   of the year

When Monday Night Football
   is finally here.

Season after season,
   one thing's the same:

      You watch more commercials

      Than the football game!

But take heart fans,
   here's some worse news:

After all those ads,
   your team could still lose!

Actually, 2/5 of each hour of football is taken up by commercials.

How many minutes of each hour is spent with players actually playing the game?

(Remember, there are 60 minutes in an hour.)

GEOMETRY

The Big Fold

Maria had a square piece of paper that measured 8 inches by 8 inches. Maria folded the paper in half 3 times in a row. (The first two folds are shown.)

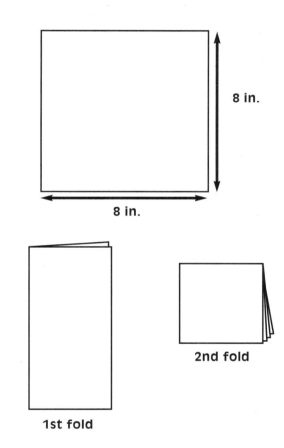

8 in.

8 in.

1st fold

2nd fold

How many rectangles did Maria end up with?

What were the length and width of each rectangle?

Use an 8- by 8-inch piece of paper to solve the problem.

17

TIME

Don't Cry Over Spoiled Milk

Ralph bought two quarts of milk fresh from the farm. He bought the first quart on September 26. It had an expiration date of October 16. Ralph knows he bought the second quart 2 weeks after the first quart, but he can't read its expiration date.

Would it be okay for him to drink this milk on Halloween night? Explain.

COMBINATIONS

Costume Combos

For Halloween, Alisha has 2 hats and 2 body suits.

How many different costume combinations can she make? Draw each combination.

Alisha just found 2 masks.

Now how many different costume combinations can she make?

GEOMETRY

The X-House

Can you make an X-House like this one? Start anywhere you like. Keep drawing without lifting your pencil or re-tracing any lines.

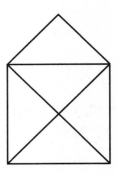

After you finish, try making an upside-down or sideways X-House. Then make this "double-roofed" X-House.

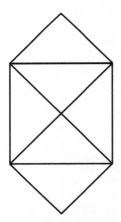

PROBLEM SOLVING

Hare and Tortoise

The hare and the tortoise ran a 40-mile race:

★ **The tortoise ran at a steady 5 miles per hour for 8 hours.**

★ **The hare ran for 1 hour at a speed of 20 mph. Then he slept for 6 hours.**

★ **After waking up, the hare ran for 1 hour, again at a speed of 20 mph.**

How much distance did each racer cover?

Who won the race?

PROBLEM SOLVING

Trick or Treat: For Hire

Leah's Trick or Treat Service takes little kids trick or treating so their parents can stay home. Leah has two basic deals:

★ **Deal 1: For $25, she'll take a whole family of kids—any size, any age—out for 2 hours. Additional hours cost $6 per hour.**

★ **Deal 2: Each kid costs $3.50 per hour.**

Suppose there are 3 kids in your family who want to trick or treat for 3 hours.

Which is the better deal?

GRAPHS

Vinnie's Halloween Haul

Vinnie counted up all his Halloween candy and made this graph. In all, Vinnie got 100 different items.

How many of them would you *estimate* were

★ **good stuff?**

★ **stuff to trade?**

★ **stuff to throw away?**

FRACTIONS

Spookeroo

Frank is writing a scary book entitled *Spookeroo*. Frank plans for the book to have a total of 48 pages. So far Frank has written 12 pages.

What fraction of the book has Frank written?

MULTIPLICATION

Trick or Treat!

Marvin wants to plan the amount of candy to give out for Halloween. He figures that he will have 25 trick-or-treaters per hour for 4 hours. Each trick-or-treater will receive 3 pieces of candy.

How much candy will Marvin need for the evening?

SPATIAL REASONING

The Waterfall

Geena and Gino both took a hike to the same waterfall named Turtle Falls. But they took different paths to get there.

★ Geena: I started at the Trail Head, passed a gas station, and went through a swamp. Then I finally arrived at Turtle Falls.

★ Gino: I started at the Trail Head and also passed a gas station. I didn't see any swamp. I went through a cave before coming to Turtle Falls.

Complete the map below to show how Geena and Gino arrived at the waterfall. Draw in features of the map. Show the routes.

MIXED OPERATIONS
Ronnie's Book

To celebrate Halloween, Ronnie is reading his favorite book, *Spook Out!* In 3 hours, Ronnie has read 45 pages of the book.

If he continues reading at the same rate, how long will it take Ronnie to read the entire 180-page book?

PROBLEM SOLVING
The Unknown Pumpkins

The pumpkins shown balance perfectly on the scale.

★ The weights of Pumpkins A and D are shown.

★ Pumpkin C is half the weight of Pumpkin D.

Find the weight of Pumpkin B.

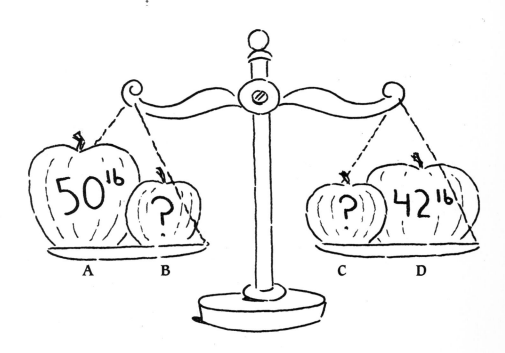

NOVEMBER

FRACTIONS
Fraction Show-Down

Which fraction is larger?
Write a < or > sign in the box.

1/9 ☐ 1/10

Explain how you arrived at your answer.
Draw a picture if you need one.

GEOMETRY
Try a Triangle

How many different triangles can you make using 9 one-inch long wooden matchsticks?
Use matchsticks or paper strips to make your triangles.

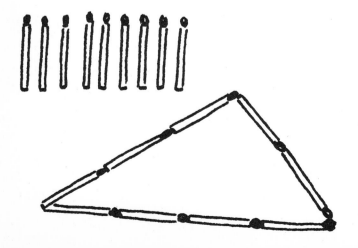

PROBLEM SOLVING
Election Day

In the November 3rd election for dogcatcher, 1,000 people voted. The results are shown below:

**Aaron:
450 votes**

**Baerga:
350 votes**

**Calloway:
200 votes**

Suppose Calloway drops out of the race and another vote is taken between Aaron and Baerga.

How many of Calloway's 200 votes must Baerga get so that she and Aaron will be tied?

MIXED OPERATIONS

Giant Thanksgiving Meatball

Instead of turkey, Vinnie decided to cook a giant meatball for Thanksgiving. A 12-pound meatball takes 3 hours to cook.

At this rate, how long would it take to cook a 20-pound meatball?

TIME

Gloomy November

Darcy kept track of the weather in November. He found that there were just as many Crummy days as Forget-About-It days, and the same number of Okay days as Yucky days.

If there were 10 Crummy days, how many Okay days were there?

(HINT: There are 30 days in November.)

FRACTIONS

Butterball Pizza

Every November, our family
always EATS A

Creation we call the
Butterball PIZZA.

It looks like a pizza with
cheese and tomatoes,

But it's topped with turkey
and mashed potatoes,

Gravy and cranberries,
stuffing piled high —

It's a Thanksgiving dinner
on a pizza pie!

So if you like Thanksgiving
Italian style,

Our Butterball Pizza
will make you smile!

This Butterball Pizza weighed 40 ounces when it was whole.

How many ounces of the pizza would you estimate are left?

MONEY

The Great Garbanzo

The Great Garbanzo can not only read people's minds, she can also see into their pockets. An audience member had $100 in $1 bills, $5 bills, $10 bills, and $20 bills. In all, there were 11 bills in his pocket. "I can see into your pocket," the Great Garbanzo says. "I can tell you exactly what bills you have."

Can you "see" into the audience member's pocket as well? Which 11 bills did the audience member have?

GEOMETRY

Tile It

Which one of these tiles can you use to completely cover this floor without any gaps or overlaps?

Make your own tiles out of paper to show your answer.

Floor

Tile 1   **Tile 2**   **Tile 3**

Tile 4

PATTERNS

Area Patterns

What happens when you double the length and width of a square? Does its area also double?

To find out, compute the area of each square. Record your data in the data table.

Square	Area
1 x 1	
2 x 2	
4 x 4	
8 x 8	

What pattern do you see?

By how much does the area increase each time?

FRACTIONS

Thanksgiving Trip to Fannie's Grannie

Once a year,
the family of Fannie

Drives to visit
their dear old Grannie.

After their journey
is 3/5 over

They stop for lunch
in a town called Dover.

If the entire trip
is 100 miles—no more—

How far is Dover
from Grannie's front door?

MONEY

No Change Betty

Betty has $1.05 in coins, but she cannot give change for a dollar, a half-dollar, a quarter, a dime, or a nickel.

What coins does Betty have?

MULTIPLICATION

Doggie Olympics

The Doggie Olympics are held at Woof Stadium every November. Woof Stadium has 8 sections. Each section has 40 rows with 25 seats in each row.

How many seats does Woof Stadium have?

PROBABILITY
PB&J Spill

Reggie is carrying a tray that contains 48 open-faced peanut butter and jelly sandwiches. If Reggie trips on a banana peel and all the sandwiches go flying,

★ **how many sandwiches would you expect to land peanut-butter-side up?**

★ **how many sandwiches would you expect to land peanut-butter-side down?**

FRACTIONS
Dumbest Movie of the Year

Three movies were nominated for the Dumbest Picture of the Year: *The President's Hair Is on Fire, Duh!,* and *The Cheese Diaries. The President's Hair Is on Fire* got 1/3 of the vote, *Duh!* got 3/8 of the vote, and *The Cheese Diaries* received the rest of the votes.

Which movie won the award?

LOGICAL REASONING
Digit Puzzle

Each digit in this equation has been replaced by a letter. Find each digit. Write the correct digits in the spaces provided.

(HINT: The number 5 has been provided as a clue.)

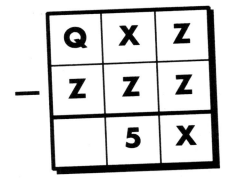

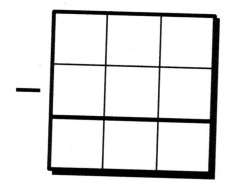

TIME

Day 16

Thanksgiving Late and Early

Each November, Thanksgiving falls on the last Thursday of the month.

What is the earliest date on which Thanksgiving can fall?

What is the latest date on which Thanksgiving can fall?

STATISTICS

Day 17

Chamiqua's Streak

She's a basketball star,
  Chamiqua Moore.

How many points did
  Chamiqua score?

23 points,
  and then 15,

Followed by 11,
  with 26 in between.

There was one final game
  for Chamiqua Moore.

How many points
  did Chamiqua score?

Chamiqua had a scoring average of 20 points per game over 5 games.

How many points did she score in her final game?

FRACTIONS

Day 18

Shocked and Amazed

Follow the steps below. Use a calculator. You will be *shocked* and *amazed* by your answer!

1. **Choose any number greater than 1,000.**

2. **Find 1/2 of the number.**

3. **Find 1/2 of the number you ended up with in step 2.**

4. **Find 1/2 of the number you ended up with in step 3.**

5. **Multiply the number you ended up with in step 4 by 8. What number do you get?**

TIME

All Lined Up

At 12 noon on November 21st, the hour hand and the minute hand of the clock line up precisely.

How many more times will the two hands line up precisely by 12 midnight?

At what times will they line up?

MEASUREMENT/GEOMETRY

Down the Garden Path

What is the area of the garden inside the white path?

What is the area of the white path around the garden?

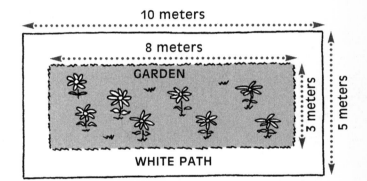

DECEMBER

MEASUREMENT

Let There Be Lights

To bring holiday cheer
   on holiday nights,

Michelle is stringing up
   holiday lights.

Red, yellow,
   green, and blue—

So many colors!
   So much to do!

Michelle wants to string lights all around the front of the house and around all windows and doors that face the front.

How many feet of wire will she need?

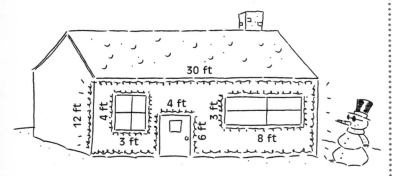

PATTERNS

Professor Snooper on the Case: A Puzzling Pattern

An archaeologist asked Professor Snooper to help interpret this mysterious number pattern that he found in an old Egyptian stone ruin.

Professor Snooper determined that each number in the pattern is the sum of the two previous numbers.

What is the first number in the series that is greater than 100?

GEOMETRY

Skyscraper Message

Each year during the holiday season people display their initials on the Sky Tower skyscraper by lighting up different rooms in the building.

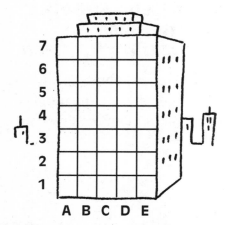

Show how you would display your own initial on the tower.

Which rooms would be lit up and which rooms would be left dark? Identify each room using its floor number and room letter.

DIVISION

Paul's Push-Up Bet

Coach Parker bet Paul that he couldn't do a total of 200 push-ups in 4 days. Paul took the bet. He did the same number of push-ups from December 9 to December 12, for a total of 200 push-ups.

How many push-ups did Paul do each day?

P.S. Because he lost the bet, Coach Parker had to wear this cap for one week!

MIXED OPERATIONS

Dog So Slender: The Spa for Dogs

Is your dog a touch on the chunky side?
Does it waddle and sway when it walks?
Then come to Dog So Slender
Your pooch will be slim as a fox.

Yes, come to Dog So Slender
Your pooch will be stylish and sleek.
We guarantee to our customers
Their dogs will lose 3 pounds a week.

Eddie the cocker spaniel weighs 56 pounds.

If he follows the program starting on December 3rd, how much is Eddie likely to weigh on December 31st?

PROBABILITY

Roland's Rollin'

To see whether it was time to clean his room, Roland rolled a die.

★ **If Roland rolled a 4, he would clean his room right away.**

★ **If Roland rolled a 5 or a 6, he would clean his room later on that day.**

★ **If Roland rolled a 3 or less, he would clean his room the next day.**

When was Roland most likely to clean his room?

MEASUREMENT/GEOMETRY

Box of Cubes

Philippa stacked 40 small cubes in the Big Box. The cubes filled the Big Box exactly.

What is the width of the Big Box?

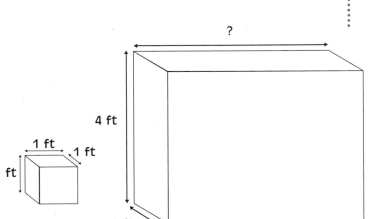

DIVISION

Faucet Man Saves the Day

Help! The faucet in Morgan's basement was dripping. Faucet Man to the rescue! Faucet Man plugged the leak fast. Morgan was saved!

The leak filled a gallon jug in 3 hours.

If Faucet Man hadn't come, how many gallons would have been lost in one 24-hour day?

ADDITION

Magic Square

Complete this magic square. Every row, column, and diagonal of three numbers should give a sum of 18.

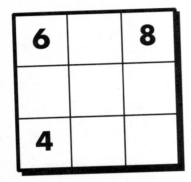

MONEY

The Z-1000 Music Madness CD Club

Is music your thing? Then the Z-1000 Music Madness CD Clubs are for you. There are two different clubs to join:

★ **Z-1000 Hot Hits Club:** Each CD costs $10.

★ **Z-1000 Freebie Club:** Each CD costs $12. Every 5th CD is free.

If you bought 10 CDs, which deal would be better?

What if you bought 14 CDs?

GRAPHS

pizza.com

pizza.com is an Internet company that delivers a delicious-looking "virtual pizza" to any computer in the world. This graph shows closing stock prices for pizza.com on the stock market.

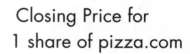

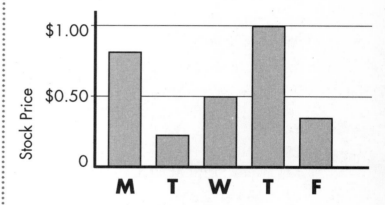

If you had 100 shares of the stock, on which days was your stock worth

★ **more than $50?**

★ **about $50?**

★ **less than $50?**

★ **about $100?**

DIVISION

Cross-Country Ski Racer

The Cross-Country Ski Race had two legs that were 24 km and 36 km in length. Gretchen finished the first leg in 2 hours. She finished the second leg in 3 hours.

What was Gretchen's average speed for the entire race?

PROBLEM SOLVING

Professor Snooper on the Case: A Missing Number

News Flash! A well-known number has turned up missing. Professor Snooper is on the case. Here are her clues. Can you find the missing Mystery Number?

★ The original Mystery Number was doubled.

★ Then the doubled total was tripled.

★ Then 10 was added to the tripled total to get a final total of 100.

What was the original Mystery Number?

FRACTIONS

The Acorn Log

Friends, do the squirrels on your gift list
Seem tired of seeds and nuts?
Then give them a genuine ACORN LOG
From the folks at J.J. Lutz.
They're made of wood and sawdust
And chopped-up acorn meats
And a lot of other indigestible things
That only a squirrel could eat.
So this year, friends, be generous
And really go whole hog.
Give your squirrels what they want:
A genuine Acorn Log!

Each Acorn Log is made of 5 oz of sawdust, 4 oz of tree bark, and 6 oz of acorns.

What fraction of the Acorn Log is actually made of acorns?

MEASUREMENT/GEOMETRY

Me Flag

How would you like a flag with your own picture on it? Get the "Me Flag" from Flaggers Incorporated. A Regular "Me Flag" measures 6 feet by 4 feet. To get a Jumbo "Me Flag," increase the length and width of the Regular Flag by 1 foot in each direction.

How much greater is the area of the Jumbo flag?

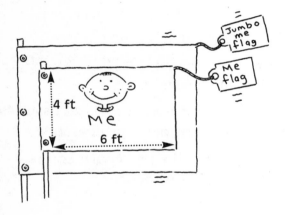

TIME

Electronic Pets

Tanya got two electronic pets for the holidays. Their names are Taki and Maki.

★ **Taki needs to be fed once every 6 hours.**

★ **Maki needs to be fed once every 8 hours.**

Both pets feed at exactly 12 noon on December 26.

At what date and time will both pets feed again at the exact same time?

PERMUTATIONS

Carolers

Mariel, Barry, Kyle, and Erica are going caroling. They're not sure how to position themselves. All they're certain of is that Barry, the tallest caroler, should stand on the left.

In how many different orders can they stand if Barry stands on the left? List each order.

DECIMALS/FRACTIONS

Fish-Off

Wilson has two fishes—Suzie and Murray. Suzie weighs 2.36 ounces. Murray weighs 2 3/8 ounces.

Which fish weighs more?

How much more does it weigh?

MEASUREMENT

Old Rat Cheese

Ralph gives Old Rat brand cheese for gifts. To wrap Old Rat Cheese, Ralph leaves the square ends of the package open so the cheesy aroma can enter the room.

How long should the paper be to cover the sides of the gift exactly and leave the ends open?

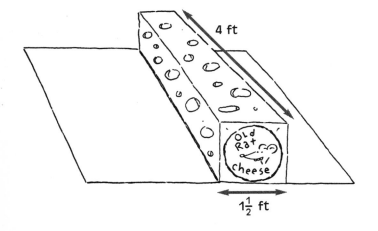

MONEY

Four Ugly Sweaters

Oliver received four ugly sweaters as gifts. He wants to exchange 3 of them for a pair of cool sneakers that costs $59.95. But if the total amount of the sweaters he returns is more than the price of the sneakers, the store will not refund the difference.

Which 3 sweaters should Oliver return so he can get the sneakers and lose the least amount of money?

JANUARY

TIME

Party Time!

Get out your party hats! In exactly 240 seconds the New Year will begin.

What time is it right now?

What day is it?

ADDITION

Cold Spell

Brrr! January can get so cold. So far, the coldest day of the year had a daybreak temperature of 12 degrees below zero. By noon, the temperature had warmed up to 8 degrees above zero.

By how many degrees had the temperature risen since daybreak?

DECIMALS

Mary, Mary

Mary, Mary,
   quite contrary,

Is your
   calculator clean?

"Oh yes," said Mary,
   quite contrary,

"It went through
   the washing machine!

"It seems okay,
   except today

When I multiplied
   0.3 by 0.2

The answer on the screen
   was clear and clean.

But it seemed too small
   to be true!"

Mary's calculator says the product of 0.3 and 0.2 is SMALLER than either of the numbers she multiplied.

Is Mary's calculator broken? Explain.

MONEY/FRACTIONS

Singles Shoe Store

Welcome to Singles,
  the shoe store with sole.

At Singles we have only
  one single goal:

Here you can buy
  shoes one by one.

That's half the shoes,
  but twice the fun!

Pick any shoe,
  right off the shelf.

At Singles each shoe
  is sold by itself.

Match a left sneaker
  with a right slipper,

One with Velcro,
  the other with a zipper.

Singles—the shoe store
  that gives you more fun.

The store that sells shoes,
  one by one.

Singles is having a "Buy 1 Shoe for 1/4 Off, Get a Less Expensive Shoe for 1/2 Off" sale.

How much will this mismatched pair of shoes cost?

PROBLEM SOLVING

Bridge Lanes

Inspector Hector works in Lane 1 at the Wheatstone Bridge.

Poor Inspector Hector! No one seems to like his lane. Only 2 cars are lined up in his lane, while 7 cars are in Lane 2, and 6 are in Lane 3.

How should the cars move over so that all three lanes have the same number of cars?

GRAPHS

What Vegetables?

Mitch likes pizza a lot—perhaps too much. He made this graph of his diet.

What fraction of the time does Mitch eat cheese pizza?

P.S. How can Mitch improve his diet?

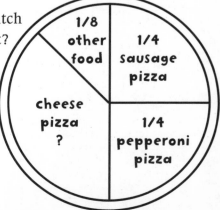

TIME

And Now, This Word

On channel 7, the Monday Night Movie shows shampoo commercials every 16 minutes. On channel 9, Monday Night Bowling has a pretzel commercial every 12 minutes. At 8:00 P.M., both programs show a commercial.

What time will it be when they both show a commercial at the same time again?

STATISTICS/COMBINATIONS

Minnie and Mike

Minnie and Mike
    waited tables

In a place
    called Mr. Widget's.

When Mike asked
    for Minnie's phone number

She wrote down
    a series of digits.

But when Mike went home
    and got on the phone

The digits were smeared—
    and now Mike feared

His chance to call Minnie
    had disappeared.

Mike can read the first 6 digits in the number as: KL5-678. But he doesn't know what the last digit is.

How many numbers would Mike need to call to be sure that he reaches Minnie? List the numbers.

TIME

The Rusty Old Cuckoo Clock

In the attic, Bree found a rusty old cuckoo clock that ran fast. The clock gained an extra 15 minutes every hour. Bree set the correct time on the clock at exactly 12 noon. Later that day Bree came back. Her watch (which was correct) said 4:00.

What time did the cuckoo clock have?

PROBLEM SOLVING

The Shovelin' Life

Got snow? Rina's Super-Duper Speedy Snow Service will get rid of it—fast!

RINA'S SUPER-DUPER SPEEDY SNOW SHOVELING SERVICE

Sidewalk $7

Driveway $10

Special: Sidewalk/
Driveway Combo $15

Rina made $66 last weekend.

What kinds of shoveling jobs did she do?

(Note: Rina did at least one of each kind of job.)

GEOMETRY

The Big Triangle

How many triangles can you find in the figure at right?

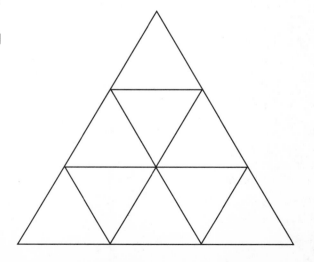

PROBLEM SOLVING

The Master Flipper

Rex wants to become a Master Burger Flipper at Burger Town. To pass the Master Flipper test, Rex must cook everything on the menu so they all get done at the exact same time.

★ **Jumbo Burgers take 3 1/2 minutes to cook.**

★ **French fries take 6 minutes to cook.**

★ **Junior Burgers take 2 minutes to cook.**

★ **Meta Burgers take 2 1/2 minutes to cook.**

In what order should Rex cook each item?

How long should he wait between items?

GEOMETRY

The Big Triangle, Part 2

How many parallelograms can you find in this figure?

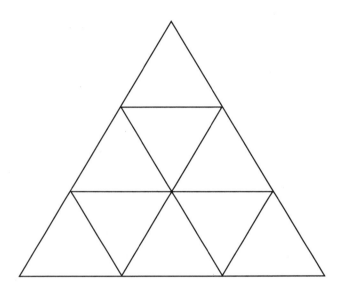

FRACTIONS

The Fifteenth

On January 15, the month of January is 15/31 complete.

Is the month more than half over or less than half over on January 15? Explain how you know.

DIVISION

Mungo, the Great, and the Sneeze

Mungo the Great is a circus performer who rides on an elephant while he divides numbers. Mungo was dividing a number when the elephant sneezed and Mungo forgot what the number was. He does remember that he divided the number by 7 and got a quotient of 34 with a remainder of 3.

What number did Mungo divide?

$$7\overline{)\,?\ ?\ ?}\qquad 3\ 4\ R\ 3$$

PATTERNS

Bits of Bytes

In computers, bits of data are called *bytes*. One thousand bytes is equal to 1 kilobyte, or 1 KB. Fill in the blanks below.

1 KB =	1 x 1,000 =	1,000 bytes	
10 KB =	10 x 1,000 =	10,000 bytes	
100 KB =	100 x 1,000 =	_____ bytes	
1,000 KB =	1,000 x 1,000 =	_____ bytes	
		or 1 megabyte	

How many bytes are in 1 megabyte?

 NUMBER OPERATIONS

Fives are Wild

Use any of the four operation signs (addition, subtraction, multiplication, or division) to make the four 5s below equal to 2.

5 ☐ 5 ☐ 5 ☐ 5 = 2

Use parentheses to show how the numbers are grouped.

 MEASUREMENT/GEOMETRY

Rectangles and Perimeter

Both rectangles below have the same area.

12 cm

6 cm

8 cm

_____ cm

What is the height of the second rectangle?

Which rectangle has the larger perimeter?

What is its perimeter in centimeters?

Day 19 — PATTERNS

Pattern Squares

Find the pattern in the squares below. Complete the square by filling in the missing numbers.

1 →	2 →	4 →	8 ↓
128 ←	←	32 ←	16
256 →	→	1024 →	↓
←	←	←	

Day 20 — MONEY

Gordo Goes to the Movies

Gordo went to the movies to see Harry the Horse in his new blockbuster hit, *The Horse Who Became Vice President*. Gordo brought a $20 bill to the movie. He bought a ticket for $7.00, and came home with $7.02 in change.

What refreshments did Gordo buy at the movie?

Multiplex 500 Theater

Tickets. $7.00
Small popcorn . . . $2.25
Medium Popcorn . . . $3.49
Jumbo popcorn . . . $4.25
Ice Cream Bar $3.10
Medium Drink $2.49
Jumbo Drink $3.25

FEBRUARY

MEASUREMENT

Sara's Magnificent Mile

Sara organized her Magnificent Mile Skateboard Race around this square track.

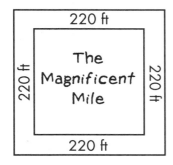

How many laps must the skateboarders complete to go 1 mile?

(HINT: 1 mile = 5,280 feet)

MULTIPLICATION

The Heart Month

How many times will your heart beat on Valentine's Day?

To find out, measure the number of times that your heart beats in one minute. Use your 1-minute heart rate to calculate how many times your heart beats in:

★ one hour

★ one 24-hour day

★ the entire month of February

Use a calculator to find your answers.

MEASUREMENT

The Great Valentine's Day Race

Joe and Juan had a crush on Evonne.

So when they thought they saw her
   wave from across the pond

And cry out "HELP!" the race was on!

Joe dove in the water, Juan went
   on land.

When they reached Evonne,
   she held up her hand

And said, "Stop, you two,
   you don't understand.

I never said HELP — that wasn't my cry.

When I waved my hand,
   I was just saying HI."

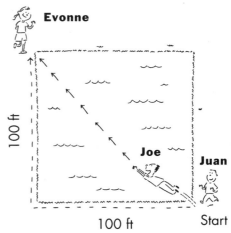

Who went farther to meet Evonne— Joe or Juan?

How much farther?

Solve this problem using a model.
Measure each distance.

PATTERNS

Spiraling Boxes

Look at the pattern below. How many rectangles are in Level 4? Count them and fill in the table.

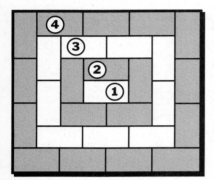

Level 1	1
Level 2	5
Level 3	9
Level 4	
Level 5	
Level 6	

Predict: How many boxes would be in Level 5? Level 6? Write your answers in the table.

MIXED OPERATIONS

Tennis Anyone?

A tennis player named Mort
Showed great style when playing
  his sport.
He looked unbelievably great,
Hitting 80 balls straight,
Except none of them landed
  on the court.

A case of tennis balls contains
12 cans with 3 balls in each can.

If Mort buys balls by the case, how many cases does he need to have 100 balls?

How many extra balls will Mort have?

FRACTIONS

Marty's Tree

Marty planted a tree seed outside his bedroom window, which is 30 feet above the ground. The tree grows at a rate of 1 1/2 feet per year.

How long will it take the tree to reach Marty's window?

PROBLEM SOLVING

Soup's On!

Lucinda makes Glurk Soup by mixing 3 types of soup together.

8 oz   15 oz   10 oz

Lucinda made exactly 64 ounces of soup.

How many cans of each type of soup did she use?

(HINT: She used at least one can of each type of soup.)

MIXED OPERATIONS

Princess Regina's Castle

Princess Regina is stuck in a castle tower that is 40 feet above the ground. The Princess can escape using a ladder made out of bed sheets tied together. Each bed sheet is 6 1/2 feet long. However, tying the sheets together uses up 1 1/2 feet of each sheet.

How many sheets does the Princess need?

LOGICAL REASONING

Stuck on Rainbow Island

Fox, Rabbit, Turtle, and Chicken are stuck on Rainbow Island with only one rowboat. The rowboat holds only 2 animals at a time. Rabbit and Chicken cannot be left alone with Fox.

How can all 4 animals get off the island?

PROBLEM SOLVING

Mr. Cupid's Valentines

Roses are red,

Violets are blue.

Need a good Valentine?

I'll write one for you!

My name is Mister Cupid,

My Valentines are unsurpassed.

Just pay me $7.50

And I'll write one for you fast.

Mr. Cupid charges $7.50 for a 4-line Valentine poem. Each additional line costs $1.50.

How much will a 10-line Valentine cost?

MULTIPLICATION

The Steps, Part 1

These 4 steps climb a total height of 6 feet.

How many steps would it take to climb a height of 30 feet?

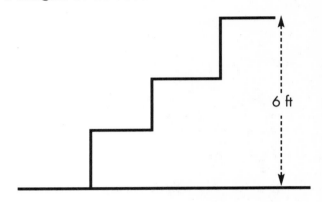

6 ft

TIME

Old King Joel

Old King Joel was a rock-and-roll soul

And a rock-and-roll soul was he.

He waved his hand

And called for his band

And they played 'til half past three.

King Joel and his band played for 2 hours and 20 minutes, and stopped at 3:30 A.M.

At what time did they start playing?

FRACTIONS

The Steps, Part 2

An ant must climb both the front and top of each step. The front of each step measures 1 1/2 feet high. The top of each step also measures 1 1/2 feet across.

How far does the ant travel to reach the top of the steps?

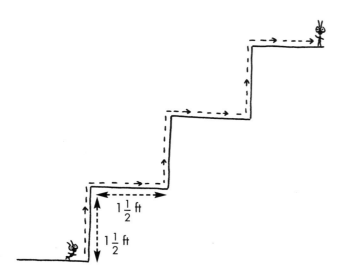

GEOMETRY

Baby Toy

Jake's baby sister Wanda is rolling a 5-sided baby toy over the table. Each side of the toy measures 4 inches. Wanda pushes the toy ahead one side at a time.

How many pushes will it take to roll the toy off the edge of the table?

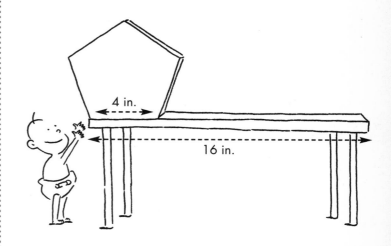

PERMUTATIONS

Scrabble-On

Marta has these letter tiles in Scrabble.

How many different arrangements can she make?

How many are actual words?

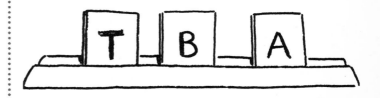

FRACTIONS

Going for the Record!

Yikes! Harry read about a man in the *Guinness Book of World Records* whose fingernails were several feet long! Harry's nails grow at a rate of 1/8 inch per week.

How long would Harry's nails get if he let them grow for 1 year?
(HINT: There are 52 weeks in one year.)

LOGICAL REASONING

Drawer Puzzle

Winston keeps his dresser drawers very well organized.

★ **The sock drawer is 4 drawers above the pants.**

★ **The sweater drawer is just above the pants.**

★ **The underwear drawer is just below the socks.**

Where is Winston's shirt drawer?

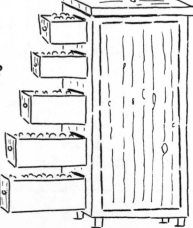

DECIMALS

Gone Fishin'

Louie went fishing at Lake Louise.

★ **Louie's fishing rod is 5 feet long.**

★ **The distance from the tip of the rod to the water surface is 18.4 feet.**

★ **Louie's fishing line reaches 37.6 feet down into the water.**

★ **The reel on Louie's pole still holds 60.5 feet of fishing line all wound up on a spool.**

How long is the entire fishing line?

5 ft

18.4 ft

37.6 ft

ESTIMATION

Know That Spout!

You can identify different kinds of whales by their spouts.

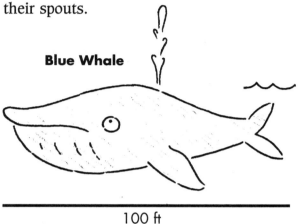

Blue Whale

100 ft

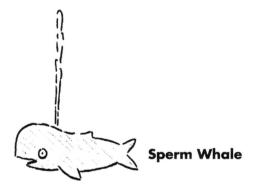

Humpback Whale

Sperm Whale

Right Whale

Use the blue whale's length to estimate the length of each whale. Then estimate the height that its spout reaches.

PATTERNS

Make a Pattern

Study these patterns.

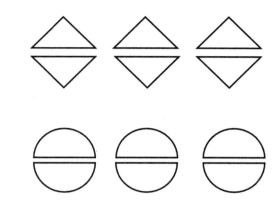

Use this figure to make a pattern that is similar to the patterns above.

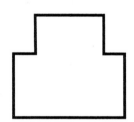

MARCH

FRACTIONS

Game Day

Roberto shaved his head when he joined the swim team on March 1. Roberto's hair grows at a rate of 2/5 inch per month.

How long will his hair be on September 1 when the swim season ends?

PROBLEM SOLVING

Migration

Spring is the time when many animals migrate to their northern homes. Gray whales travel from Baja, California, to the Bering Sea in Alaska to feed in the spring—a distance of 4,850 miles. Golden plover birds migrate 1,500 miles farther than gray whales, going from Brazil to northern Canada.

In one round trip, how far do golden plovers travel in all?

TIME

Sam in March

by Rachel

In like a lion,
Out like a lamb—
Like my baby brother,
His name is Sam.
When he wakes up
He's loud and funny.
But two hours later
He's quiet as a bunny.

In one 24-hour day, Sam took 4 naps for:
★ 3 hours, 25 minutes,
★ 4 hours, 2 minutes,
★ 2 hours, 58 minutes, and
★ 4 hours, 11 minutes.

How long was Sam awake?

LOGICAL REASONING

Go Fly a Kite

Muffy, Carlos, Doug, and Shay are flying kites.

★ **Muffy's kite is 75 feet higher than Carlos's kite.**

★ **Doug's kite is 25 feet higher than Carlos's kite, but 75 feet lower than Shay's kite.**

★ **Carlos's kite is 100 feet from the ground.**

How far off the ground is each kite?

PERMUTATIONS

Kickball All-Stars

Abra, Bennie, Carla, and Dean are playing kickball.

"I want to be up first!" cries Abra.

"No, me!" says Bennie.

"No, me!" shouts Carla.

"I want to be up *last*," says Dean.

How many different kicking orders can you think of for the four players if Dean is up last? List each order.

FRACTIONS

Billy and Sue's Canoe

Billy and Sue shared a canoe.

They were the best of friends.

They had a fight—neither felt right.

And here the friendship ends.

Now what to do with the canoe?

"Split it in half," says Billy.

Sue rolls her eyes. Then she cries:

"That idea is just plain silly."

Even though the idea was silly, Billy and Sue split the 14-foot canoe into two pieces. Billy's piece was 6 3/4 feet in length.

How long was Sue's piece?

NUMBER OPERATIONS
Magic Boxes

Roses are red,
Violets are blue.
Fill in the magic boxes
To make this equation true:

$$51 \;\boxed{}\; 3 = 13\tfrac{1}{2} \;\boxed{}\; 3\tfrac{1}{2}$$

Write a +, –, x, or ÷ sign in each box.

DECIMALS
Jeff's Odometer

The odometer on Jeff's bike isn't accurate. Every time the odometer registers 1 mile, Jeff has really only traveled 0.8 of a mile. The odometer now reads an even 100 miles.

How many miles has Jeff really traveled?

PROBLEM SOLVING
Rocky Mountain High

The tree line at Chester Mountain is at 10,500 feet above sea level. Above this altitude, there are no trees. Tara's group hiked along Chester Trail, starting at 9,750 feet. The trail went up by 1,025 feet, then dipped down 650 feet. Tara's group then climbed 440 feet before having lunch.

Were there any trees to shade the group from the sun during lunch?

MEASUREMENT

Hamburger Heaven

Jo and Mo went to Burgerville

And ordered a bucket of grub.

Their burgers and fries came out
  super size

And arrived in a giant tub.

The hamburgers weighed in
  at 28 ounces

And came in a cardboard box.

As for the fries, they were salty
  and soggy

And heavy as french-fried rocks!

Jo and Mo each got a 28-ounce burger and 20 ounces of french fries.

How many pounds did their bag weigh?
(HINT: 1 pound = 16 ounces)

PROBLEM SOLVING

Slide Ride

Rona wants to ride the Alpine Slide Ride at Chester Mountain.

Alpine Slide Ride
1-hour pass $8.50
4-hour pass $24.00
8-hour pass $36.00

How much does Rona save per hour by buying an 8-hour pass instead of a 4-hour pass?

Suppose Rona plans to ride the Slide Ride for 5 hours. What pass or passes should she buy to save the most money?

GRAPHS

March Weather

Snowfall for Chester Mountain is shown in this graph.

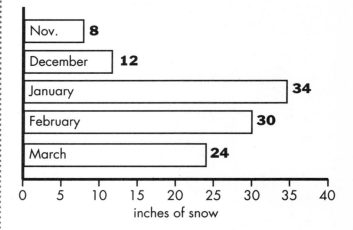

inches of snow

How many total inches of snow fell over the 5 months shown?

Which months got more snow than March? Less snow?

Which two months together got exactly half of the year's total snowfall?

MAPS

Canoe for Two

Lulu and Jake want to paddle their canoe from Cape Hook to Ball Isle.

Give directions for how they can make the trip from the X on Cape Hook to the Z on Ball Isle.

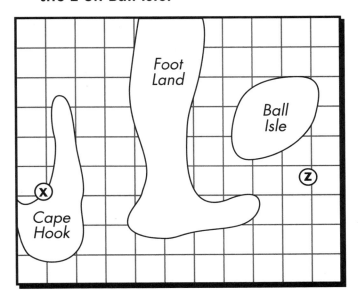

Key

100 yd = ☐

North

For example, you might start out by saying, "Go north 400 yards." Each square on the map measures 100 yards on a side.

PROBLEM SOLVING

The Turtle and the Toad

The turtle and the toad were having a race to see who was slower.

"I'm the slowest animal in the forest," said Turtle. "I run 100 feet in 4 hours."

"I'm slower than you," said Toad. "I run 72 feet in 3 hours."

Who is slower?

How do you know?

GEOMETRY

The Impossible Triangle

One of the three triangles described below is "impossible."

Which one is it? How can you fix this triangle so that it is not impossible?

★ **Triangle A: 4 inches by 5 inches by 6 inches**

★ **Triangle B: 4 cm by 4 cm by 4 cm**

★ **Triangle C: 3 inches by 3 inches by 7 inches**

Use a ruler and strings, strips of paper, or other real objects to solve this problem.

PERMUTATIONS
Scrambler

Deena is having trouble unscrambling a word with these 3 letters.

G P I

How many different arrangements of the 3 letters can you make?

What is the word?

TIME
Hikers

Darcy, Jed, and Alma want to plan a 2-day hike in March on Chester Mountain.

★ **Darcy is free from March 1 to March 10.**

★ **Jed is free from March 5 to March 15.**

★ **Alma is free from March 9 to March 18.**

On what dates should the three hikers schedule their hike?

STATISTICS
In Like a Lion, Out Like a Lamb

The average temperature for the final 5 days of March was exactly 10 degrees warmer than the average temperature for the first 5 days. The average temperature for the first 5 days of March was 40 degrees. Temperatures for the last 4 days of the month were 54 degrees, 43 degrees, 45 degrees, and 59 degrees.

What was the temperature of the final day of the month?

PROBLEM SOLVING
Dorinda for Hire

Dorinda the Clown charges the following rates for parties.

★ **$15 basic fee**

★ **$2.50 extra for each special juggling trick**

★ **$3.25 extra for each special unicycle trick**

★ **$2.00 extra for each trick done with a dog balancing on her head.**

How much would Dorinda charge for 3 juggling tricks, 4 unicycle tricks, and 2 of those tricks done with a dog balancing on her head?

MEASUREMENT
Mel and Marti's Thirsty Party

Mel and Marti had a picnic party
On March the twenty-first.
They had a fine lunch but forgot
  the fruit punch
And soon they were dying of thirst.
But they were in luck when
  a lemonade truck
Drove by and had a freak spill.
They held out cups as lemonade
  shot up
And soon they drank their fill.

Forty-two gallons of lemonade spilled on the road.

How many cups of lemonade spilled?
(HINT: There are 16 cups in a gallon.)

APRIL

DECIMALS

Circus Seesaw

Bernie and Berty, the performing seals, are riding a seesaw with Marlene the bear and Nicky the baby bear.

Which way will the seesaw tilt?

Who will go up?

Who will go down?

PROBLEM SOLVING

A Cool Hundred

How can you make a sum of $100 out of $20 bills, $10 bills, and $5 bills, using exactly 10 bills?

Make sure to use at least one of each kind of bill.

DECIMALS

April Soil

In the spring, here's the thing:
The water must come first.
April showers bring May flowers.
The soil must quench its thirst.

It rained 4 times in the first 10 days of April, bringing 1.2, 0.35, 0.67, and 1.04 inches of rain.

In all, how many inches of rain fell?

FRACTIONS

Cool Dude

Randy loves this Cool Dude sweatshirt. But the sweatshirt costs $40 and Randy has only $12.

Next week, the sweatshirt will go on sale for 1/4 off the regular price. Next month, the sweatshirt will go on clearance sale where it will sell for 1/2 off the sale price.

How much more money will Randy need to buy the sweatshirt during the clearance sale?

DECIMALS

Box Office Blitz

The top 3 movies for the first week of April were *Shoes 'n' Socks, April Fool,* and *Gross-Out Friday.* Ticket sales are shown in the graph.

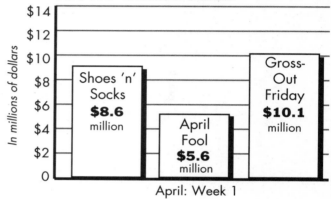

During the second week of April, *Shoes 'n' Socks* gained $1.4 million in ticket sales, *April Fool* gained $4.6 million, and *Gross-Out Friday* lost $0.8 million.

What was the top-grossing movie for the second week?

The lowest-grossing movie?

TIME

Professor Snooper on the Case: The VCR Mystery

Nancy watched the movie *Shoes 'n' Socks* on her VCR. The movie lasted 1 hour and 45 minutes. At the end of the movie, the meter on the VCR read +1:30.

What was the reading on the meter when the movie began?

FRACTIONS

Day 7
Chunky Chili Cheese Cracklin' Corn Chips

One 12-ounce jar of Fetzer's new All-Natural Chunky Chili Cheese Cracklin' Corn Chips are made of all natural ingredients:

★ **Mashed Mush:** 1 oz

★ **Cracked Corn:** 4 oz

★ **Dried Drippings:** 1 oz

★ **Boiled Oil:** 2 oz

The rest of the recipe is made of Chili Cheese Chunks.

What fraction of the 12-ounce mixture is made of Chili Cheese Chunks?

MEASUREMENT

Day 8
Enter the Dragon

The Komodo dragon from the East Indies measures 2.8 meters.

What is the approximate length of the Komodo dragon in centimeters?

(HINT: 1 meter = 100 centimeters)

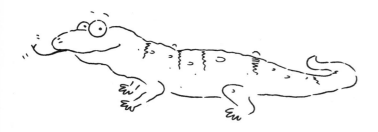

PROBLEM SOLVING

Day 9
Musical Fractions: Clara's Song

Clara is composing a song using half notes (♩), quarter notes (♩), and eighth notes (♪). Each section, or measure, of the song contains notes that add up to 1 whole note. For example, the first measure below has a half note, an eighth note, a quarter note, and another eighth note:

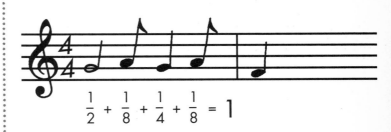

$$\frac{1}{2} + \frac{1}{8} + \frac{1}{4} + \frac{1}{8} = 1$$

How can you finish the second measure song by adding 2 more notes?

3 notes?

4 notes?

Remember, the sum of each measure should equal 1 whole.

PROBLEM SOLVING

Whale Weight

Baby blue whales can gain 10 pounds an hour in weight by drinking their mother's milk. A baby whale weighs 1,000 pounds.

If the baby whale drinks milk for 3 straight 24-hour days, how much will it weigh?

ADDITION

Tiger's Round

Tiger Woods's golf score is shown in the chart below.

Hole	1	2	3	4	5	6	7	8	9	Total
Par Score	4	3	4	5	5	4	3	3	4	
Tiger's Score	4	2	6	4	4	3	4	3		

The par score shows how many shots the hole should take if it is well played. An under-par score indicates superb playing. An over-par score indicates poor playing.

In all, Tiger was 3 under par for all 9 holes. What score did he get on the 9th hole?

What was his total score?

MULTIPLICATION

Justin, the 7-Year-Old Fish

Justin, Judy's pet fish, is 7 years old.

How many months old is Justin?

How many weeks old is Justin?

How many days old is Justin?

PROBLEM SOLVING

Snips

Moe and Flo own the Snips Hair Parlor. Moe can finish a haircut in 20 minutes. Flo takes 30 minutes to style her customers' hair. Both Moe and Flo make the same amount of money over an 8-hour day. Moe charges $10 per haircut.

How much does Flo charge?

LOGICAL REASONING

Professor Snooper on the Case: Murray's Birthday

Murray the Turtle forgot the date of his own birthday. He hired Professor Snooper to find out the date.

★ **His birthday occurs some time during the second half of April.**

★ **The number of the day is divisible by 7 but not by 4.**

On what date is Murray's birthday?

FRACTIONS

Tax Time

No matter how busy your business—
All those dollars, e-mails, and faxes—
Everything stops on the 15th of April.
It's time to pay your taxes!

One-fifth of Sam and Pam's $60,000 income goes to pay taxes.

How much do Sam and Pam pay in taxes?

PROBLEM SOLVING

Jeff's Monster Cookies

Jeff is baking his special monster cookies. The cookies are so big and full of chocolate chips that only 6 cookies fit on a cookie sheet. Jeff got an order to bake 30 monster cookies.

If each batch of cookies takes 40 minutes to bake, how long will it take Jeff to bake all the cookies?

MULTIPLICATION

Box Office Blitz

There once was a film star
    named Shaw,

Whose face was without any flaw.

One thing was clear:

When he gazed in the mirror

He truly enjoyed what he saw.

A movie camera takes 30 still pictures per second.

If Shaw is on the screen for 2 minutes, how many still pictures did the movie camera take?

GEOMETRY

Snug Fit

How can you fit the four L-shaped pieces into the grid below so that they completely cover the grid?

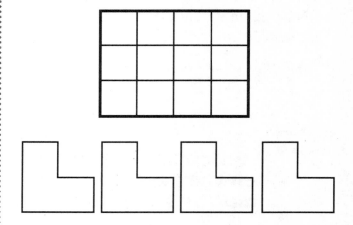

Use cut-outs or drawings to solve the problem. You can rotate or flip the pieces any way you like.

ESTIMATION

April in a Box: Perfume for Dogs

Does your dog sometimes smell

Like last month's dirty socks?

Then do yourself a favor—
   get April in a Box.

Yes, April in a Box, the perfume
   of April flowers.

Just spray it on your pooch—

No need for baths or showers!

April in a Box comes in 3 sizes:

★ Small: 2 ounces for $2.99

★ Medium: 4 ounces for $3.99

★ Large: 6 ounces for $6.99

Which size is the best value? Estimate your answer.

PATTERNS

Play Ball!

In April, the baseball season begins. Here are Barry Bonds's home-run records for the first 4 months of the baseball season:

Month	April	May	June	July	Aug.	Sept.
Home Runs	4	7	10	13		

If the same pattern continues, how many home runs will Bonds hit during September?

How many home runs will Bonds hit in all?

MAY

Day 1

PATTERNS

Backyard Garden Club

The Backyard Garden Club is making plans for its new garden. The basic pattern of roses, lilies, and tulips is shown here:

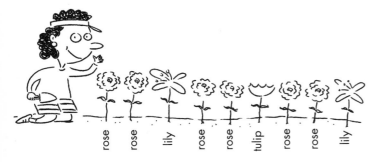

rose rose lily rose rose tulip rose rose lily

What are the next two flowers that should be planted?

The next four flowers after that?

Day 2

PROBLEM SOLVING

Dog Years

Ralphie the dog is 4 years old in human years. Each human year is equal to 7 dog years. That means that Ralphie is 28 in dog years. In human years, Penny is 3 years older than Ralphie.

How old is Penny in dog years?

Day 3

LOGICAL REASONING

Chess Championships

The year's Chess Championships include both human and computer contestants:

★ Bobby Shafto, a human, lost to the computer program Blackbeard-45.

★ Blackbeard-45 was beaten by a 10-year-old human named Suzie Q. LaRoo.

★ Quargon the Robot beat Blackbeard-45 but lost to Suzie Q. LaRoo.

Rank the contestants from first to last.

Day 4

ESTIMATION

Tall Guy

NBA All-Star Tim Duncan is 7 feet tall.

Use the Tim Scale to estimate the height of the following in feet:

★ **Sniffy, the dog**

★ **Sasha, the 5th grader**

★ **Milton, the math teacher**

★ **Rex, the horse**

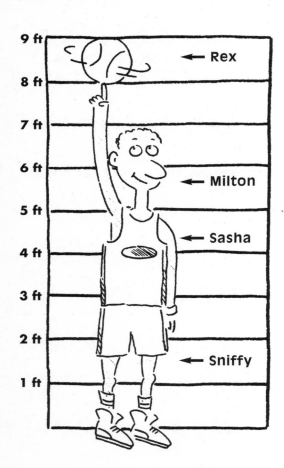

Day 5

PATTERNS

Hexagon Colors

This figure is made of 6-sided shapes called hexagons.

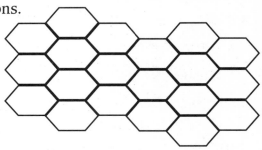

Color the figure using red, blue, green, and yellow so that no two neighboring hexagons have the same color.

Day 6

SUBTRACTION

Dinkins the Dog

There once was a young dog
    named Dinkins,

Who excelled at intelligent thinkin'.

When asked by her master,

"What's the capital of Nebraska?"

She replied, "Lincoln"
    without even blinkin'.

The drive from Lincoln, Nebraska, to Cleveland, Ohio, going through Chicago covers 1,007 miles. Cleveland to Chicago measures 354 miles.

How far is it from Chicago to Lincoln?

72

PATTERNS
Geo-Series

Draw the next figure in this group.
(HINT: Count how many sides each figure has.)

PROBLEM SOLVING
Puffball Donuts

The Puffball Donut shop starts the morning with 80 donuts on hand.

★ **The shop sells 40 donuts per hour on average.**

★ **The shop makes 20 new donuts each hour.**

At this rate, by the end of how many hours will the shop have run out of donuts?

MIXED OPERATIONS
All-You-Can-Eat

The After School Club is sponsoring an All-You-Can-Eat Hotcake Breakfast. The hotcake recipe calls for 3 scoops of hotcake mix to make 12 hotcakes.

How many scoops of hotcake mix will the club need to make 144 hotcakes?

LOGICAL REASONING

Sluggers

The South Side Sluggers softball team was trying to figure out its opening lineup:

★ "Action" Ackley bats after "Bigfoot" Baxter and before "Calamity" Cruz.

★ "Dangerous Dan" Dexter bats before "Action" Ackley and after "Bigfoot" Baxter.

★ "Egghead" Easley bats just before "Calamity" Cruz.

Find the batting order of the first 5 players of the Southside Sluggers.

PROBLEM SOLVING

White Water

In still water, Barbara can paddle her kayak at a speed of 4 miles per hour. Traveling down the Russian River, Barbara is aided by a 2-mph current.

What will Barbara's speed be when she paddles from Start to Endpoint?

What will her speed be when she returns to Start in the opposite direction?

How long will it take Barbara to reach Endpoint from Start?

How long will it take Barbara to return from Endpoint to Start?

DECIMALS

Mr. Muscle's Dilemma

Mr. Muscle's dumbbell is unbalanced. One side of the dumbbell weighs 94.6 pounds.

How many 8.6-pound weights should Mr. Muscle put on the other side to balance the dumbbell?

2 mph current

PROBABILITY

Spin 2 Sale

Each year Wendy's World of Sneakers has its "Spin 2 Sale." During this sale, customers spin the spinner to see how much to pay for shoes.

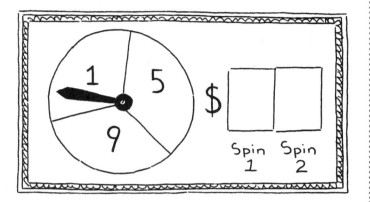

To participate, spin the spinner twice and write each number in the box provided.

What is the most you can pay for your sneakers? The least?

What are the chances that you will pay more than $90 for your sneakers? Less than $20?

FRACTIONS

The Pencil and the Pen

The pencil and the pen,
  now and again,

Will differ in what they think.

"It's all in the lead," the pencil said.

But the pen said, "It must be
  the ink!"

A pen was half empty after it had written 250 pages. A pencil was 1/3 used up after it had written 200 pages.

How many pages can each write?

Which writes more?

PATTERNS

Squares and Circles

Observe the series of figures.

    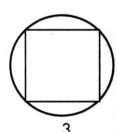

1   2   3

**What will figure 4 look like?
Draw a picture.**

75

DIVISION

The End of Harry Potter

Margo has 75 pages left to read in her *Harry Potter* book.

If Margo finishes the book in 5 hours, how many pages will she have read in each hour, on average?

PROBLEM SOLVING

The Dogfish Song

A dogfish by the name of Clark
Liked to swim every night
   until dark.
When a catfish swam by
He would let out a cry
Which I swear, sounded just like
   a bark!

The catfish weighs 1 pound less than twice the weight of the dogfish.

If the catfish weighs 21 pounds, how much does the dogfish weigh?

PATTERNS

There Were Bells

The church bells chime out the time using this coded system.

Real Time	Bell Time
2:00	Dong dong
2:15	Dong dong ding
2:30	Dong dong ding ding
2:45	Dong dong ding ding ding
3:00	Dong dong dong

What time would it be when the bells ring out, "Dong dong dong dong ding"?

What pattern would the bells ring at 6:30?

TIME

Cup a Joe

At the Hot Pot Coffee Shop, the waiters make a new pot of regular coffee every 15 minutes. Every 24 minutes they make a new pot of decaffeinated coffee. The shop opens at 6:00 A.M. with a new pot of both regular and decaf coffee.

When is the next time a new pot of each type of coffee will be made together?

NUMERICAL REASONING

Ping-Pong

Thirty-two players entered the Ping-Pong tournament. In the first round, all 32 players will play. In the second round, the 16 winners from the first round will play each other.

How many rounds will the tournament need to crown a champion?

JUNE

LOGICAL REASONING
The Ice Stand

The Ice Stand had 3 ice pop flavors: chocolate, vanilla, and strawberry. Burt, Gert, and Curt each got a different-flavored pop.

★ **Curt did NOT get strawberry or chocolate.**

★ **Gert got either chocolate or vanilla.**

Which flavor did each person get?

DIVISION
The United States of Jenny

Jenny designed her own flag—the United States of Jenny. It has 10 stripes, because Jenny is 10 years old.

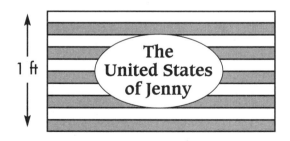

The United States of Jenny

1 ft

Jenny wants to make her flag 1 foot high.

How many inches high should she make each of the 10 stripes?

TIME
Wedding Bell Blues

There once was a young girl
  named Kate,
Who had trouble keeping track
  of the date.
She kept on forgetting
'Til she missed her own wedding,
But by then it was simply too late.

Kate's wedding was supposed to take place

★ **in the summer;**

★ **during a month with 30 days;**

★ **on the fifth Saturday of the month;**

★ **on a date that is a prime number.**

What was the date of Kate's wedding?

PROBLEM SOLVING

Professor Snooper on the Case: The Lost Combo

J. Jefferson Jackal was issued the combination for his pool locker and immediately forgot all three numbers. He hired Professor Snooper to find the combination.

★ The first number is 3 times the second number.

★ The second number is 5 more than half of 14.

★ The third number is 7 more than the second number.

Professor Snooper used the clues above to find the combination.

What is J. Jefferson Jackal's locker combination?

PROBLEM SOLVING

Horse for Hire

Peggy plans to make money over the summer by selling $10 rides on her horse Edwin. Edwin can ride for 1 hour at a time. After each ride, Edwin needs a 45-minute rest.

What is the greatest amount of money Edwin can make each day if he starts at 9 A.M. and stops riding by 5 P.M.?

PROPORTIONAL REASONING

Summer Trip

June is planning a summer vacation trip from Washington, D.C., to San Francisco, California. Each inch on the map represents 1,000 miles. The distance from Washington, D.C., to San Francisco on the map is about 2.5 inches.

About how many miles is it from Washington to San Francisco?

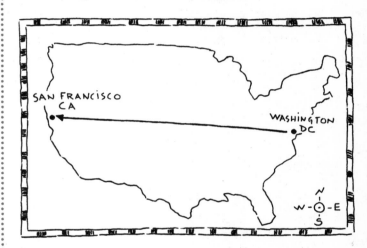

PATTERNS

Figure Series

Observe the series of figures.

A　　**B**　　**C**　　　**D**

Complete figure D so that it will fit in with the series. Draw a picture.

MIXED OPERATIONS

Heat Wave

At 8:00 A.M., the temperature was 78 degrees. By 2:00 P.M., the temperature had risen 14 degrees. By 9:00 P.M., the temperature had dropped 16 degrees.

What was the temperature at 9:00 P.M.?

ESTIMATION

Trail Blazers

The Trail Blazers' Club wants to blaze a new trail to the Trading Post that goes through the woods.

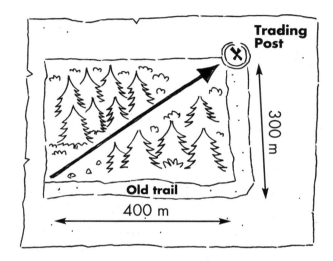

How much shorter will the new trail be than the old trail? Use a model to estimate your answer.

DECIMALS

Dripper

In one minute, a leaky faucet dripped a total of 0.033 liters.

How many liters would it leak in

★ **1 hour?**

★ **one 24-hour day?**

★ **one 365-day year?**

TIME

Movie Fone

Phil had only 2 hours—between 6:30 P.M. and 8:30 P.M.—to see a movie. He called Movie Fone and found out the following information:

★ *Attack of the Green Globs* started at 12 noon and had continuous showings all day. Each showing lasted 1 hour and 45 minutes.

★ Continuous showings of *Senator Lummox* started at 12:40 P.M. Each showing lasted 1 hour and 30 minutes.

Which movie should Phil go to? Explain your answer.

GEOMETRY

Quadrilaterals

A quadrilateral is a 4-sided figure.

How many different quadrilaterals can you make by connecting the dots in the grid below? Two sample quadrilaterals are shown.

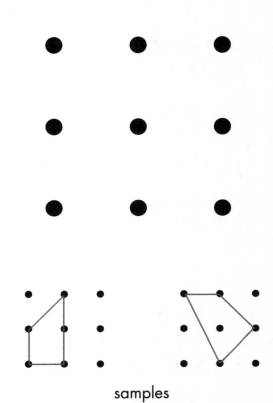

samples

PROBLEM SOLVING

The Cane Toad

The cane toad can lay up to 30,000 eggs at a time. Only about 50 out of every 1,000 eggs survive to adulthood.

How many cane toads would you expect to survive after a female laid a full batch of 30,000 eggs?

LOGICAL REASONING

Fossil Mess

A collection of fossils and their labels got mixed up at the Museum.

Use the facts below to figure out how many millions of years ago each dinosaur lived.

★ The Iguanodon lived 40 million years before the Protoceratops.

★ The Diplodocus lived 20 million years after the Iguanodon and 70 million years before the Tyrannosaurus.

★ The Tyrannosaurus lived 5 million years before the Triceratops, which lived about 65 million years ago.

PROBLEM SOLVING

Jupiter's Sun

It takes about 8 minutes for light to travel from the sun to Earth—a distance of 93 million miles. Jupiter is 484 million miles from the sun.

How long would it take light from the sun to travel to Jupiter?

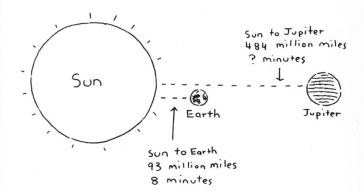

GEOMETRY

Giant Smiles and Frowns

Gus wants to paint a giant smiley face on his driveway. Gail wants to paint a giant frowny face.

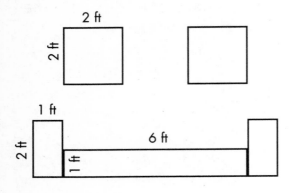

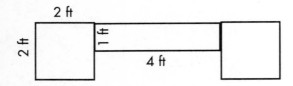

Which figure will use up less paint?

How many fewer square feet will it have?

MAPS

Earthquake

An earthquake was detected at Station A, Station B, and Station C on this map of Butternut County.

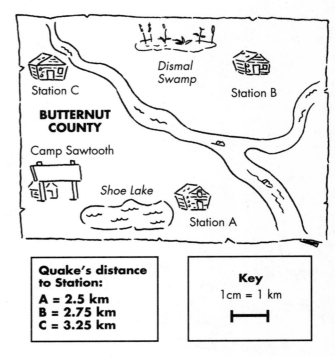

Quake's distance to Station:	Key
A = 2.5 km	1cm = 1 km
B = 2.75 km	
C = 3.25 km	

Where is the quake's center?
To find out:

★ Draw a circle around each station with a radius that matches its distance to the quake in centimeters. *(Measure from the center of each station's door.)*

★ The quake's center will be located where the 3 circles meet.

FRACTIONS/DECIMALS

The Wrench of the Three Bears

Goldilocks stopped at the Three Bears' house to find a wrench to fix her motorcycle.

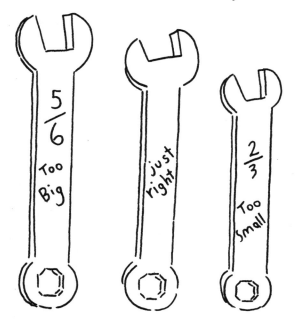

Papa Bear's 5/6-inch wrench was too big! Mama Bear's 2/3-inch wrench was too small! Somewhere in the tool box was Baby Bear's wrench—and it was the perfect size!

What do you think was the size of Baby Bear's wrench? Write your answer as a fraction or a decimal.

PROBLEM SOLVING

Squirrel-Away Fence

Friends, are the squirrels in your yard
Really becoming a pest?
Do they chatter away, night and day,
And never allow you to rest?
Then get the Amazing
    Squirrel-Away Fence.
It'll stop them right in their tracks.
If you aren't DELIGHTED with
    Squirrel-Away Fence
Then we'll DOUBLE your money back!

Each Squirrel-Away Fence comes complete with Squirrel Repellent and fence posts that are spaced 10 yards apart.

How many fence posts will a 100-yard straight fence have?

DIVISION

The Most Under 30

The number 12 can be divided evenly by 12, 6, 4, 3, 2, and 1. Each of these numbers is a factor.

What number under 30 has the most factors?

ANSWERS

SEPTEMBER

1. Any female name starting with the letter L, such as Linda or Liza

2. Answers will vary. Wendy can use combinations such as four 5¢ stamps; one 5¢ stamp and five 3¢ stamps; or five 2¢ stamps and two 5¢ stamps.

3. The bone is about 3 times Walter's height, or about 12 feet long.

4. 4 jumps. After the third jump Hoppy will be 9 feet up the log. On the fourth jump she'll reach 14 feet and be over the end.

5. Earliest starting date is September 2nd; latest is September 8th.

6. Answers will vary. The simplest solution is for Natasha and Doris to each give one acorn to Boris.

7. The Cheapo pencil for 10¢, the Deluxe pen for 98¢, and the Cheapo notebook for 89¢ totals $1.97. Suvi will get 3¢ in change.

8. September 15th

9. 1/3

10. Rey ate ice cream first. Then, he bought a new shirt. He got a haircut last.

11. 2 dimes, 1 nickel, 2 pennies

12. 15 bags

13.

8	9	7
7	8	9
9	7	8

14. 4:55 PM

15. 7 kids won a mystery book; Mia, Barb, and Beth each won a T-shirt; Rex won a book and a plush toy, but not a T-shirt

16.

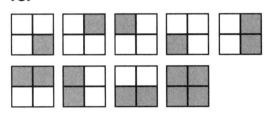

17. 1 in 5 chances that Rennie will pull out a polka-dot sock; 4 in 5 chances that he'll pull out a striped or white sock.

18. Both bakers are correct. Amounts will vary.

19.

	2	5	0
+	2	5	0
	5	0	0

20.

```
         10              30
  o──────●───────────────────────o
Clarksville  Albion          Brentwood
```

OCTOBER

1. 51 minutes

2. Winnie made $12, Pat made $4, and Vinnie made $9.

3. 5 vans

4. 11 seeds each for breakfast, lunch, and dinner

5. 70 days

6. 15; 21; 28

7. 10 pumpkins

8. 36 minutes

9. 8 rectangles each measuring 4- by 2-inch

10. No. The expiration date for the first quart was 20 days after it was bought, so the second quart would most likely expire on October 30.

11. Alisha can make 4 combinations with 2 hats and 2 suits. With 2 masks, she can make 8 costume combinations.

12.

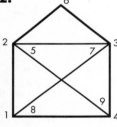 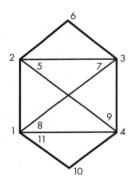

13. Both racers covered 40 miles. The race was a tie.

14. Deal 1 is the better deal. It costs $.50 less than Deal 2.

15. About 50 items were "Good Stuff"; 25 were "Stuff to Trade"; and 25 were "Stuff to Throw Away."

16. 1/4 of the book

17. 300 pieces of candy

18.

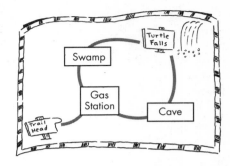

19. 12 hours

20. Pumpkin B = 13 lbs

NOVEMBER

1. >

2. 3 triangles: 1 x 4 x 4, 2 x 3 x 4, 3 x 3 x 3

3. Baerga needs 150 out of 200 votes, or 3/4 of the votes that Calloway received.

4. 5 hours

5. 5 Okay days

6. 24 ounces

7. 5 $1 bills, 1 $5 bill, 4 $20 bills, and 1 $10 bill

8. Tile 4

9. Area increases 4 times each time the sides are doubled.

10. 40 miles

11. Answers will vary. A sample response may be 1 half-dollar, 1 quarter, and 3 dimes, or 1 dollar coin and 1 nickel.

12. 8,000

13. 24 face-up and 24 face-down

14. *Duh!* won. *Duh!* got 9/24 of the vote, *The President's Hair Is on Fire* got 8/24, and *The Cheese Diaries* got 7/24.

15.

	6	0	5
−	5	5	5
		5	0

16. The earliest date for Thanksgiving would fall on Nov. 24, while the latest date would fall on Nov. 30.

17. 25 points

18. The same number that you started out with

19. 11 more times at 1:06 P.M.; 2:11 P.M.; 3:17 P.M.; 4:22 P.M.; 5:27 P.M.; 6:33 P.M.; 7:38 P.M.; 8:43 P.M.; 9:49 P.M.; 10:54 P.M.; 12 midnight

20. The area of the garden is 24 square meters, while the white path is 26 square meters.

DECEMBER

1. 140 feet of wire

2. 144

3. Answers will vary.

4. 50 push-ups each day

5. 44 pounds

6. Tomorrow; 3 or less is the most likely result.

7. 5 feet

8. 8 gallons

9.

6	4	8
8	6	4
4	8	6

10. For 10 CDs, the Freebie Club is the better deal—$96 as opposed to $100 in the Hot Hits Club. For 14 CDs, the Hot Hits Club is the better deal—$140 as opposed to $144 in the Freebie Club.

11. More than $50 on Monday and Thursday; about $50 on Wednesday; less than $50 on Tuesday and Friday; about $100 on Thursday

12. 12 kilometers per hour

13. 15

14. 6/15 or 2/5

15. 11 square feet

16. 12 noon on December 27

17. 6 orders: Barry, Mariel, Kyle, Erica; Barry, Mariel, Erica, Kyle; Barry, Kyle, Mariel, Erica; Barry, Kyle, Erica, Mariel; Barry, Erica, Mariel, Kyle; and Barry, Erica, Kyle, Mariel

18. Murray weighs 0.015 ounces more.

19. 6 feet

20. The $32.50 sweater, the $11.95 sweater, and the $15.95 sweater

JANUARY

1. 11:56 P.M. on December 31st

2. 20 degrees

3. No, her calculator is not broken. 0.3 x 0.2 = 0.06, which is smaller than either number.

4. $33

5. Answers will vary. A sample response may be to move 1 car from Lane 3 and 2 cars from Lane 2 to Lane 1.

6. 3/8

7. 8:48 P.M.

8. 10 numbers: KL5-6780, KL5-6781, KL5-6782, KL5-6783, KL5-6784, KL5-6785, KL5-6786, KL5-6787, KL5-6788, KL5-6789

9. 5:00

10. 3 sidewalks, 3 driveways, 1 sidewalk/driveway combo

11. 13 triangles

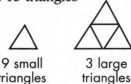

9 small
triangles

3 large
triangles

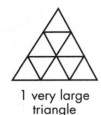

1 very large
triangle

12. Start with fries. Wait 2 1/2 minutes then flip on the Jumbo. Wait 1 minute then flip on the Meta. Wait 30 seconds then flip on the Junior.

13. 15 parallelograms

3 diamond
parallelograms

6 small
parallelograms

6 large
parallelograms

14. Less than 1/2

15. 241

16. 100,000; 1,000,000; 1,000,000

17. Answers may vary. A sample response might be (5 ÷ 5) + (5 ÷ 5) = 2.

18. 9 cm; the 6 x 12 rectangle has the larger perimeter, which is 36 cm.

19.

1	2	4	8
128	64	32	16
256	512	1,024	2,048
32,768	16,384	8,192	4,096

20. A medium popcorn for $3.49 and a medium drink for $2.49

FEBRUARY

1. 6 laps

2. Answers will vary.

3. Juan went about 60 ft farther than Joe.

4.

Level 1	1
Level 2	5
Level 3	9
Level 4	13
Level 5	17
Level 6	21

5. 3 cases with 8 balls leftover

6. 20 years

7. 1 can of black bean soup, 2 cans of noodle soup, and 3 cans of pea soup

8. 8 sheets

9. Answers will vary. A sample response may be: Turtle takes Fox to the other island and drops Fox off. Turtle returns and picks up Chicken. Chicken drops off Turtle and returns to pick up Rabbit. Chicken and Rabbit return to the other island.

10. $16.50

11. 20 steps

12. 1:10 A.M.

13. 12 feet

14. The toy will roll off on the 4th push.

15. 6 arrangements: ABT, ATB, BAT, BTA, TAB, TBA. 2 arrangements are actual words: BAT and TAB.

16. 6 1/2 inches

17. 3rd drawer down

18. 121.5 feet

19. Blue Whale: Length = 100 ft, spout = 40 ft
Humpback Whale: Length = 50 ft, spout = 13 ft
Right Whale: Length = 30 ft, spout = 15 ft
Sperm Whale: Length = 45 ft, spout = 45 ft

20.

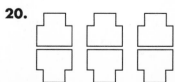

MARCH

1. 2 2/5 inches

2. 12,700 miles

3. 9 hours, 24 minutes

4. Shay's kite is 200 feet off the ground; Muffy's is 175 feet; Doug's is 125 feet; and Carlos's kite is 100 feet.

5. 6 orders: Abra-Bennie-Carla-Dean; Abra-Carla-Bennie-Dean; Bennie-Abra-Carla-Dean; Bennie-Carla-Abra-Dean; Carla-Abra-Bennie-Dean; and Carla-Bennie-Abra-Dean

6. 7 1/4 ft

7. 51 ÷ 3 = 13 1/2 + 3 1/2

8. 80 miles

9. No; they were at 10,565 feet, which is above the tree line.

10. 6 pounds

11. Rona saves $1.50 per hour; for 5 hours, Rona should buy the 4-hour pass and one 1-hour pass for a total of $32.50.

12. 108 inches of snow fell over the 5 months. January and February got more snow than March, and November and December got less snow. February and March got 54 inches, which is half of the year's total snowfall.

13. Answers will vary. A sample answer may be: Go north 400 yards. Go east 200 yards. Go south 600 yards. Go east 600 yards. Go north 300 yards. Go west 200 yards. Go north 300 yards. Go east 300 yards.

14. Toad is slower at 24 feet per hour. Turtle runs 25 feet per hour.

15. Triangle C is impossible because the 2 short sides don't meet. To fix the triangle, make one or both of the short sides longer, e.g., 3 inches by 5 inches by 7 inches.

16. 6 different arrangements: PIG, PGI, GIP, GPI, IPG, IGP. The word is PIG.

17. March 9 and March 10

18. 49 degrees

19. $39.50

20. 672 cups

APRIL

1. The seesaw will tilt toward the seals, pushing the bears up and the seals down.

2. Answers will vary. A sample answer may be 7 $10 bills, 1 $20 bill, and 2 $5 bills, or 2 $20 bills, 4 $10 bills, and 4 $5 bills.

3. 3.26 inches

4. $3

5. Top-grossing movie is *April Fool,* and the lowest-grossing movie is *Gross-Out Friday*.

6. −0:15

7. 4/12 or 1/3

8. 280 cm

9. 2 notes: 1 half + 1 quarter; 3 notes: 1 half + 2 eighths or 3 fourths; 4 notes: 2 eighths + 2 quarters.

10. 1,720 pounds

11. On the 9th hole, he scored 2. His total score is 32.

12. 84 months; 364 weeks; 2,555 days

13. $15

14. April 21st

15. $12,000

16. 200 minutes or 3 1/3 hours

17. 3,600 still pictures

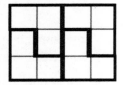

18. Answers will vary.
A sample answer may be:

19. The medium size is the best value.

20. 19 homers in September; 69 homers in all

MAY

1. Rose, rose; the next four flowers would be tulip, rose, rose, and lily.

2. 49 years old

3. 1st place: Suzie Q. LaRoo, 2nd place: Quargon, 3rd place: Blackbeard-45, 4th place: Bobby Shafto

4. Sniffy is about 1.5 ft tall; Sasha is about 4.25 ft tall; Milton is about 5.75 ft tall; Rex is about 8.5 ft tall

5. Answers may vary. A sample solution may be:

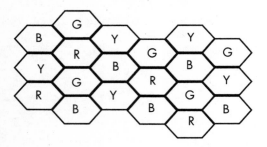

6. 653 miles

7. A 7-sided figure

8. 4 hours

9. 36 scoops

10. "Bigfoot" Baxter, "Dangerous Dan" Dexter, "Action" Ackley, "Egghead" Easley, "Calamity" Cruz

11. 6 mph; 2 mph; 2 hours; 6 hours

12. 11 8.6-lb weights

13. The most you can pay for sneakers is $99; the least is $11. The chances that you'll pay more than $90 are 1/3; less than $20 are 1/3.

14. The pen can write 500 pages, while the pencil can write 600 pages. The pencil writes more.

15. Most common answer:

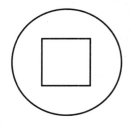

16. 15 pages

17. 11 pounds

18. 4:15; Dong dong dong dong dong dong ding ding

19. 8:00 A.M.

20. 5 rounds

JUNE

1. Curt got vanilla, Gert got chocolate, and Bert got strawberry.

2. 1 1/5 inch

3. June 29

4. 36-12-19

5. $50

6. Estimates may vary, but should be about 2,500 miles.

7. Most common answer:

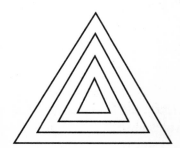

8. 76 degrees

9. The new trail should be about 200 m shorter than the old trail.

10. 1.98 liters in 1 hour; 47.52 liters in 1 day; 17,344.8 liters in 1 year

11. Phil should go to *Senator Lummox* because it starts at 6:40 and ends at 8:10. *Green Globs* starts at 7:00 and ends too late, at 8:45.

12.

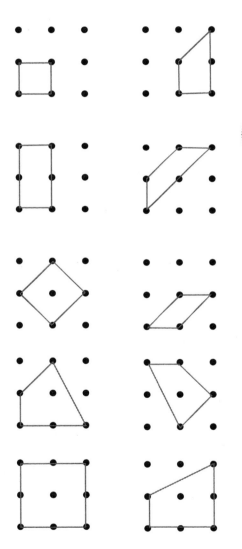

13. About 1,500 cane toads

14. The Iguanodon lived 120 million years ago; the Protoceratops about 80 million years ago; the Diplodocus about 140 million years ago; the Tyrannosaurus about 70 million years ago; and the Triceratops about 65 million years ago.

15. About 41 minutes

16. At 14 square feet, the giant frowny face is 4 sq. ft. smaller than the smiley face.

17.

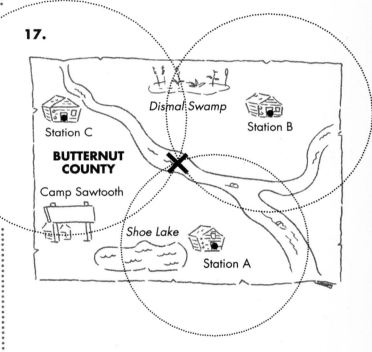

18. Answers will vary, but should be close to 3/4 or 0.75 inch.

19. 11

20. The number 24 has 8 factors: 24, 12, 8, 6, 4, 3, 2, 1